Advance Praise for *Dog Days*

Dog Days takes us back to awkward days of adolescence – managing our bodies, loving strangers and estranged parents, worshipping fallen heroes. Pedersen invokes the power of poetry, with expert line control and vivid memories, to understand what it all meant, and means, to be authentically human – to be as good as a dog.

Ken Hada - *Come Before Winter*

A unique look under the hood of conventional American upbringing and how a young man struggles to find a meaningful adult self in a world besotted with greed and cynicism.

Paul Austin, author of *Notes on Hard Times*

Dog Days

Poems and Art
by
S. Pedersen

FINE DOG
PRESS

ISBN: 978-1-955478-23-6

Printed in the United States of America
Cover and interior art by Steven Pedersen
Published by Fine Dog Press, August, 2024

FOR ALL TYKES

CONTENTS

Across the Tracks

I had a dream last night
I helped God unwrap a new bike
as he was watching tv and
painting in a small run-down apartment
next to a dumpster full of abandoned doors.

My ex-girlfriend was sitting on the couch,
eating leftover barbeque. Ribs to be exact.
Somebody changed the channel and God was upset,

Are you going to make me watch this station?

The channel was promptly changed back.

There was a news report about the greatest songs ever written.
Second place had bombs and nuclear blasts.
First place was "Hey Jude."
And God chimed in saying,

It always will be.

Twelve Lines of Chorus

Nah nah nah na'na-na nah. Na-na-na nah, hey dude.
Nah nah nah na'na-na nah. Na-na-na nah, hey dude.
Nah nah nah na'na-na nah. Na-na-na nah, hey dude.
Nah nah nah na'na-na nah. Na-na-na nah, hey dude.
Nah nah nah na'na-na nah. Na-na-na nah, hey dude.
Nah nah nah na'na-na nah. Na-na-na nah, hey dude.
Nah nah nah na'na-na nah. Na-na-na nah, hey dude.
Nah nah nah na'na-na nah. Na-na-na nah, hey dude.
Nah nah nah na'na-na nah. Na-na-na nah, hey dude.
Nah nah nah na'na-na nah. Na-na-na nah, hey dude.
Nah nah nah na'na-na nah. Na-na-na nah, hey dude.
Nah nah nah na'na-na nah. Na-na-na nah, hey dude.

By Window

So much time is wasted upon looking out windows that one might wonder what is better than leaves tossed in branches that wave in tandem to passing clouds contrasted by blue roofs over whom and whatnots stuck in rooms tucked away by painted walls and hollow desks illuminated by dull lights buzzing by power plants in distant corners controlled by dials and needle points marking measures of wattages while donuts in lounge comfort complacent worries about missed baseball games or daycare children napping absently by billing schedules and plans over forgone dreams of permission given someday that now is merely filled by looking out windows, muttering and wondering the significance before heading home.

The Good News

An old love once told me
she could never poop in public restrooms.
She wanted to avoid the splash back.

I think it is safe to say,
we all want to avoid the splash back.

I told her what I thought was common knowledge.
Just lay toilet paper in the bowl
to cushion the plop and limit the splash
—a shit-shield of sorts.

In all the years we were together
this small gift seemed to be significant,
more so than others.

Drivers Ed

I was in 9th grade and standing at the bus stop
when Chris, a neighborhood friend,
decided to attend school and offered to share
his joint wrapped in Bible paper with me.

I had no idea about the paper, or the words,
I just took a deep breath and inhaled
wanting to find a way to limit the distractions
of first period, Drivers Ed, with Mr. McCollum.

I was slightly annoyed after a couple puffs.
The hit was rough around the edges.
He just laughed and shared his ingenuity
of biblical dexterity in joint rolling.

The ride to school was bumpy as always,
but felt good, tossed to-and-fro on faux leather
ripped around the seams over cushion foam seats
while I sat staring at displays of tagged obscenities.

First period started before I wanted it to,
and I did my best to hide my state from friends,
Justin and Keith—everyone in class really.
So I sat silently, observing the time pass.

Everyone was tasked with reviewing their quiz.
Keith was called to the front of the classroom.
Apparently, he received a 100% grade and
Mr. McCollum wanted to make a display of it.

"Yeah, now see this boy is motivated."

I couldn't help myself, laughter erupting,
Yeah, now see this boy is motivated.
I gave my best Mr. McCollum impersonation,
accentuating his southern drawl of speech.

I clapped my hands in applause
in a silent classroom while everyone stared,
clueless to what my motivation was.

"You! Outside, now!"

Mr. McCollum's words jolted me back to reality.
Shit, shit, shit, shit, shit, shit, shit.
He's going to know I'm high.
Everyone is going to know I'm high.

He followed me outside and left the door open
so everyone could hear his scolding.

You think you're cool?
You think you're tough?
You a big jock, aren't you?
You play sports? —what sport do you play?

I held my head low, and replied ever so meekly,

I play tennis.

The classroom erupts with laughter.

"Oh, so you a big tennis jock are you?
That's it, isn't it?
You think you're real cool."

No, sir.

The verbal lashings continued
until, thankfully, the bell rang.

I walked to my locker,
paranoid and humbled,
and thought a lot about God that day.

Lint of the Day

Like a bird's nest, where no nest should be,
I daily pinch my bellybutton to remove the lint.
Sometimes I toss it in the trash, or if the lid is up,
the toilet bowl for it to float along before the flush.
It's a burden of sorts, such as shaving and plucking hairs.
But I do it all the same, as some things should be done.
Even now, as I write this, I know below my undershirt,
every motion made traps a little more, like a hairy net,
collecting and storing in a dark navel hole
the lint of the day that will later be picked and tossed.

Dancing Around the Matter

My thirteenth birthday happened to be on the last day of school, before summer break.

This was the last day of elementary school, and everyone was excited for junior high.

This also happened to be the day of the 6th grade dance, and everyone planned to attend.

I made up my mind to wear my new birthday clothes, jean shorts with a stylish Stüssy shirt.

Around 4pm, I left my home to walk to the local Community Center feeling like Zach Morris.

Everyone in class was there, including all my school crushes: Cami, Kacey, Amber, and Lindsay.

That night, magic happened. All the boys were instructed to toss a shoe into one big pile.

Next, each of the girls searched through to find a shoe and we all partnered up.

Wouldn't you know it, Shannon, the most popular girl in school, chose my shoe.

Let me tell you something.

She was more than any crush. She lived in a league that existed for prom queens and cheer captains.

She was a blond bombshell in a dress with ribbons, slap bracelets, and clear jelly platform shoes.

H-e-double-hockey-stick, she has my shoe. I get to hold her hand! This is the best night of my thirteen-year-old life.

I don't recall the song now, but I remember the music was loud as we slow danced between balloons and confetti.

Our hips rubbed back and forth, and all I could think about was savoring this summer night dance.

Partway through, I notice Shannon trying to tell me something, whispering in my ear.

I couldn't hear amid the song. "I'm sorry, I can't hear you," I said. Her lips continued to move.

We swayed together, back and forth, bumping to the rhythm. She persisted for my attention.

"I can't hear you. You need to talk louder. The music is too loud," I said. And then she made it clear.

"—you have A BONER!"

The dance didn't stop, and neither did the hard-on I failed to notice, pitching outward in my shorts.

I tried to play it cool, letting her know that these are just new shorts, "They stick out like that," I said.

I tried to reposition myself, but nothing could change the situation. We kept dancing awkwardly until the song ended.

I thought my social life was officially dead after that dance. Soon, everyone would know and laugh.

But thankfully, summer was here, and no social media existed back in 1994.

On the way out that night, I looked for Shannon among the crowd, not knowing what to say.

What is there to say after a dance like that? We never really talked again. But I did see her before I left.

Out along the hallway, I saw Shannon in the distance look my way with a smile of understanding.

Through all the panic and shame of puberty, I can't help but remember this dance and her smile.

It was enough.

American Boyhood

Many places in the world
hold rituals for manhood.

The Bukusu in Kenya
celebrate a circumcision
faced bravely.

On an island in the South Pacific,
the Vanuatu build towers on land
and jump off headfirst
         —secured by the snap of a vine.

The Hamar tribe of Ethiopia
have boys climb over cattle
to prove manhood to marry.

Romans exchanged tunics,
Spartans hunted at night
and called it krypteia.

My ritual was sneaking gin
and puking in Burger King
before high school study hall.

I hid hard-ons behind textbooks.
Saw dermatologists to pop pimples,
and prescribe retinol creams.

I had my first French kiss with Crystal
after final period, P.E., before summer,
while waiting for the bus ride home.

I had my first school fight in 7th grade
during the Medieval Fair
while dressed in tights as a joker
        —in a costume my mom made.

It didn't last long.
No fists were actually thrown,
just words in a circle of bravado.

But that's the rub of it.

There were no rites of passage.
No public trials of bravery to perform.
No sweat, blood, or tears shed.

The closest moment I can remember
—when I realized I was no longer a child,
happened on a spring day outside my home.

On a Sunday morning before church
my father and I stood together for a photo
and I reached up to hold his hand.

I must have been twelve or thirteen.
He swatted it away out of disgust
before one could say, *cheese*.

I didn't know the rules had changed.

I guess it was his way of saying
welcome to the world of men,
and keep your hands to yourself.

A Turn Too Much

There is such a thing as a grindstone that just won't stop
sharpening the edge of a point till it wears away, completely.

That's the problem I see today, with all the taut and terrible
anxieties manifested over in news, notifications, and necessities.

We can't quite stop it. I think we would if we could, but maybe,
if I lean in a little more it'll do it for me, strip bone bare

breaking down bits for piecemeal to be scattered so that disasters
are distributed evenly, mealy, meekly, measuredly for all.

I converse with the lost because they have come to terms with the
vocabulary of a wrecked economy bent on breaking.

We are the weight, the stone, the grinding over and above that
crushes and pushes us all into running, running, running. Go!

Secondhand

When I was young,
it was always magic.

Now days, at my age,
it feels like clearance sales
at used clothing stores,
rummaging around with
others trying to find a fit
for something that won't
smell like mistakes & cigarettes.

What price do I list
on these old shoes?

Learning the Game

My first year of little league
I played on the A's team
down at Wayne Makin Field
next to the federal prison
where guards stand in towers
with rifles strapped bandolier-style.

Fly balls often ended up across the street
by the barbed wire fence along the perimeter
—with some balls stuck in no man's land
where guards won't allow you to reach.

Preseason requirements stated that
all players must wear jockstraps with a cup.
My father told me it was to protect the family jewels
so they don't end up the size of a grapefruit.

I didn't much care for the thought,
but I remembered coach Brenner,
—a.k.a "One-Nut Brenner,"
who everyone knew lost a testicle from a fast one.

So, I gladly accepted my new equipment.

The mothers smiled when I stepped up to home plate.
I developed an at-bat ritual like a young Bambino
crowding the plate, tapping my bat against my shoes,
then across the far side of home
—with a final tap to my crotch cup.

Coach said I had a Ted Williams swing.

It must have been a sight to behold
as a scrawny kid with an adult cup
that bulged out over home plate
—a skinny Dirk Diggler playing ball.

I still haven't figured out
if my father was being facetious
with his mixed-metaphor and
choice in purchase for my protection.

My first at bat I hit a line drive
and ran bow-legged around first base,
sliding into second, safe,
with a dirt stain curved in front of me.

I became the team's leadoff batter.

In the dugout, the guys chewed sunflower seeds
and spit out *hey batter, batter* on the bench.
I got grapefruit-jewels, I told my friend, John G.,
joking that I must have big balls with my bat in hand.

At the end of every game, win or lose,
parents handed out juice boxes and oranges,
and both sides lined up to shake hands
for sportsmanship and character building

under the purview of watchful eyes.

Hollywood

Basic Instinct was released in 1992.
By the time it came out on VHS
I was well aware of all the controversy.

During my elementary school days
my dad would drop me off with friends
as he made his early morning work commute.

Most mornings my friends would be asleep.
I would nap in their game room before school,
next to the computer with AOL dial-up.

The room had a couch by the window
and a Nintendo with a broken R.O.B. unit
in a basket, and lots of movies on shelves.

When I saw the movie case,
with Sharon Stone staring back at me,
I had to see what all the fuss was about.

At 5:30 in the morning, I took the tape,
hit eject and slipped it into the tape deck.
Fast-forward. Play. White dress. Pause.

To be honest, I did the same with *Nobody's Fool*,
1994 when Melanie Griffith gives Paul Newman
a view to remember—a view I remember.

The history of cinema can be classified
by the women of the screen willing
to embody the moves that make men gaze

and whistle.

To Have and Have Not (1944)

Lauren Bacall to Humphrey Bogart

Who was the girl, Steve?

Who's what girl?

The one who left you with such a high opinion of women.
She must have been quite a gal.

…

You know, Steve,
you're not very hard to figure
—only at times.

Sometimes I know exactly what you're going to say
—most of the time

The other times,
the other times you're just a stinker.

…

You know you don't have to act with me, Steve.
You don't have to say anything
and you don't have to do anything.
Not a thing.

Oh maybe just,
whistle.

You know how to whistle, don't you Steve?
You just put your lips together and blow.

Pete

My teammates called me Pete.
Pete for Pedersen, or Sampras,
or maybe just "for Pete's sake."

I was named team captain as a sophomore,
which gave me some responsibility,
but it was mostly just a popularity contest
and I had all my friends join the team
so it's not really something to brag about.

On bad smog days, we didn't play.
But most days were clear enough.

Playing tennis in Norco is not like
playing tennis in Newport Beach.
We were considered hicks from the Inland Empire,
raised alongside dairy farms and horse trails.

We played more for fun
than serious competition.

Afterschool practices happened on the courts
up on the east side of school by the hills.
I used to change into my clothes behind cars
because the bathrooms were too far away.

If you don't know, tennis shorts are short.
Many have a slit along the side to allow for full
mobility on the court—loose with no netting

like wearing boxers over my boxers.

After one away game, we were heading home
from Jurupa Valley and sharing the bus
with the varsity softball team.
My friend Cory and I sat near the back.

I took the aisle seat and propped my leg up
across to the other side to stretch out,
still sweating and trying to keep my testicles
from sticking to the side of my thighs.

Cory and I talked and joked about the day
and slowly began to notice the gaze of the girls
looking back to listen in our conversation,
most likely impressed by our athletic prowess.

I can't remember who pointed it out first,
but we both felt so cool in that moment,
being only sophomores in high school
and getting checked out by cute senior girls.

Later that evening, when I finally made it home,
I headed up stairs to take a shower before dinner.
I sat on the laundry basket in front of the mirror
and propped my leg up to untie my shoes.

Damn it!

In a flash of realization, I finally understood
why all the girls kept their sunglasses on.
Like a damn tree ornament dangling in full view,
my racket and balls were hanging out of my shorts.

* * *

Weeks later,
when I thought the matter was forgotten,
Cory's mother picked us up from school
and offered to drive me home.

After stepping inside, she asked,

*Are you the one
who showed his nuts
to the softball team?*

* * *

In 1998, I was known as "Pete" on the tennis court.
It was a nickname.
It was all for fun and games.
It was, I presumed, a tennis reference.

I'm not too sure anymore.

Aleutian Roots

PART 1

My mother sometimes tells stories
about the early days of her marriage
with my father, out on Adak Island
during the Cold War, 1970 something.

After flight school in Pensacola,
my dad was transferred into Intelligence
and stationed in the middle of the Bering Sea,
handling fleet navigation records with the Navy.

Adak is located towards the end of
the Aleutian Islands: population few.
There is an airstrip and a military base
and history of a failed Japanese attack.

That's about it.

So when my father decided to celebrate
his birthday party, and asked my mom
to help organize the event for everyone,
they brainstormed ideas together.

He joked about hiring a dancer to jump
out of a cake for a laugh. She convinced him
it would be funnier if he jumped out
instead. It was a big hit apparently.

She was proud of this moment

and enjoyed reminiscing.
I can't help but see the story
as an example of my inheritance.

PART 2

My father sometimes tells stories
about the early days of his marriage
with my mother, out on Adak Island
during the Cold War, 1970 something.

They met in Officer Candidate School,
Rhode Island. He thought she was cute,
after seeing her eat in the cafeteria
and they began dating before graduation.

They decided to get married quickly.
He proposed half-seriously in her dorm,
only weeks before flight school, and
surprisingly, she agreed to the adventure.

That's about it.

Short time later, as a commanding officer
on the Adak base, an earthquake was reported
off the coast of Japan, and threatened to send
a tsunami that would wipe out the island.

It was late-night winter when he got the word,
and sent my mother to the top of the hill,
up towards the highest point, with everyone else.
After securing the base he went to join them.

Halfway up the hill, minutes from
the estimated impact time, my father realized he forgot
to check whether he secured top secret documents

and diligently turned around to double-check.

I thought I was going to die in that VW bug.

PART 3

My parents sometimes tell stories
about the early days of their marriage,
when they both lived out on Adak Island
during the Cold War, 1970 something.

The stories of this place seem full
of something I never saw as a kid,
two young people trying to do right
by each other while having a little fun.

When I came along in '81, they lived
in Gilroy, CA and both appeared the part
of parents, cordial to each other at dinner
and determined to abide by norms.

That was about it.

My father changed his military status
from active to reserve duty, and began
working in a garlic manufacturing plant,
before taking us up to Yakima, WA.

He worked at Tree Top for a few years,
then Coca-Cola Foods in the City of Industry,
then Tropicana, Pepsi, Nantucket Nectars,
and a few other companies in between.

My father was let go from every job he ever had.
My mother kept the house clean and cooked.
This is the childhood I remember before

the dissolution of vows I never saw,
                     —but heard stories of.

By Any Other Name

In 1993
my father took me to a sports auction in San Diego
and bought me a birthday present.

It was a letter
written and signed by O.J. Simpson.

He signed the letter
with a *Sharpie*—large, bold—
like John Hancock.

The letter details a charity event
for Cedars-Sinai
Medical Genetics
Birth Defects Center.

Tommy Lasorda is listed as
the Master of Ceremonies.

I marveled at the letter,
and traced my finger
over his autograph
encased in plastic.

At the time, my cursive S
looked like a sailboat
in front of my name.

But Simpson's signature

was sharp, impressive,
and precise in threading his S
into impson.

I practiced matching his movement.

The next year
Nicole Brown Simpson
was murdered on my thirteenth birthday,
June 12th, 1994.

Five days later
I watched
the former Heisman
and Naked Gun co-star
make a 100-mile dash
in a white Bronco with friend
and former teammate, Al Cowlings.

It was a game we all remember,
the Juice
weaving down the freeway
while the boys in blue trailed behind
like it was the goddamn Rose Parade.

I think we all wanted to root for him,
even after the chase ended.

Good guys don't do bad things.
Good guys get featured in films,
and advertisements for Hertz and Dingo boots.
Good guys ride white horses, right?

I wanted to believe in
the O.J. I knew,
—Nordberg,
caught up in some kind of crime
that Lt. Frank Drebin would soon solve
and explain.

I was in junior high
when the verdict was read.
They stopped class
so everyone could watch the tv.

It was the "trial of the century,"
everyone said.
And no one wanted to miss
how it ends.

By this time
teams were chosen
based upon color.

People worried about riots again,
after 1992.
But the dream team of
Cochran and Shapiro
knew how to play with doubt.

Maybe it was drugs,
and a deal gone bad?
Maybe it was the old
wrong place, wrong time?
Maybe, maybe, maybe.

And yes, I too wanted to believe
and chose to ignore
the Browns and the Goldmans
while focusing on the Fuhrman theory
—as some kind of *L.A. Confidential* twist.

And then the verdict.

October 3, 1995,
Case # BA097211
"We the jury, in the above entitled action
find the defendant, Orenthal James Simpson,
not guilty of the crime of murder . . ."

*   *   *

I still have the letter.
I still sign my S like O. J. Simpson.

My signature has become my own,
but there will always be a small trace of
a time when I still believed in heroes
beyond a reasonable doubt.

Water

06:50
JAN2115Feb PB

CA CASH REFUND
NO REFILL
HI-ME-OR-CT-NY 5¢
NON-CARBONTATED

PURIFIED WATER, MAGNESIUM SULFATE,
POTASSIUM CHLORIDE, SALT. *†
*ADDS A NEGLIGIBLE AMOUNT OF SODIUM
†MINERALS ADDED FOR TASTE
PURIFIED BY REVERSE OSMOSIS

0 | | **II 499700** II | II IIII 4

0
CALORIES
PER BOTTLE

20 FL OZ (1.25 PT) 591 mL

Before I Could Speak

Crawling along the floor
listening to the mechanical
typewriter, rapt by letters
terrorizing the page to
print words together by
ink, fingers, spacebar, return.

chi-che, chi-che, chi-che, zing!

I pretended in play
to type words too,
pressing buttons in random,
listening to the machine
type magic combinations of
letters in single-file order.

chi-che, chi-che, chi-che, zing!

Freud would probably say
my motives begin here,
connecting back to being
the child that first
discovered the keys that
my mother introduced me.

chi-che, chi-che, chi-che, zing!

I remember the portable
carrying case of leather

and the black keys
with little white letters
on buttons to push
the sounds of ink.

chi-che, chi-che, chi-che, zing!

It was all terribly
exciting to play writer
and produce the sounds
of writing and believe
I too could make
something worthy of print.

chi-che, chi-che, chi-che, zing!
Chi-che, chi-che, chi-che, zing!
Chi-che, chi-che, chi-che, zing!
chi-che chi-che, chi-che, zing!
Chi-che, chi-che, chi-che, zing!
chi-che, chi-che, chi-che, zing!
Chi-che, chi-che, chi-che, zing!
chi-che, chi-che, chi-che, zing!
Chi-che, chi-che, chi-che, zing!
chi-che, chi-che, chi-che, zing!

Staining

Make no mistake,
writing is pharmacy
          pills and phrases
strung out together
seeing what feels right
          smack dab
in the mind between drags
and dregs of life
to get a narrative arc
one might cling to
          sing too
scripting aloud at night
a prayer, a chant, an ohm—
scribbled stains
whispered in lines of
plotting, as if to find
some meaning
in old photos & postscripts.

type,
          type,
                    type.
. . . .
It's all t/here.
It's all w/rite.

Evening

Light through my front door
is painted sympathies.

I linger upon the wall.

The book out of reach I could write,
but only know how to whisper.

Just might take me home.

Does it sing my song you hear,
these painted sounds in front of me?

Please don't deny my sentiment.

I confess my sins in an empty room
to strangers I once knew kindly.

It is this evening light, fading now.

Sleeping in Blue

I crawl in and pull over layers
to hear my own thoughts
breathing, softly lonely hues.

I drift in make-believe prayers
to hear my own heart
beating, softly lonely too.

I dare not mutter *sorry* anew
to hear my own mind
loathing, softly lonely you.

I wait and wade through waves
to wake for orange
dawning, softly lonely blue.

Piecemeal

I bet I know why
the Buddha has a belly.
It has taken me awhile
to gain the weight

and clue

along a few roads
by different ponds
with grass just as green
to beat around the edges
more than enough

to know

the weight is the world
swallowed whole,
and held in so that
every breath and bite
moves the day.

Rub the belly.
Feed the belly.
Lay your hands
on my belly.

Have you eaten today?

Rainmaker

I once fell for
a Southern Bell.

Jolly, Jolly

We left for mountains
and sought waterfalls.

Holy, Holy

She found the rainbow.
I found the clouds.

Folly, Folly

I learned the dance
that makes rain fall.

Growing Bark

After lightning loosens leaves
and bare limbs expose clouds,
upward glances steal my sight.

I know the pecans have fallen,
scattered on the ground
about my feet ready for picking.

            Still, I look up
searching through the branches
weathered by storm

and sway.

Gate of Glass

I was on my way with a gray-haired woman.
She was excited to see the great event,
to show it herself as my guide.

"We can't miss it, you'll see, in a few minutes."

The title was something like:
        The Moment Time Stood Still
or   When Time Stopped

The big hand and little hand were close together,
minutes apart on flyers and pamphlets nearby.

Was it a play, a film, or book release?
She made no say, only, "hurry now, we mustn't wait."

To my surprise, we entered a café at the end of a bookstore
where chocolate covered éclair pies cut in large squares are sitting
on rounded white plates behind a refrigerated window.

I'll have to try one, I think, despite the fly behind the glass
and view of an old man's bloated leg in a wheelchair.

In an instant, I knew the event she led me.

Koan

A fallen leaf
knows more about
life and death
than all humanity.

It does not struggle.
It does not resist.

It only is a
fallen
leaf.

Television

The one thing that keeps me
from losing my sanity
are the words from my mother
when I was just a child

watching tv.

"Remember,
      this is all just make-believe."

A Dog's Philosophy

DIOGENES: "Enough! Lick yourself if licks intend a due turn."

The philosopher wakes by licks of dogs circling around his wine-barrel-of-a-home off the Bay of Phaleron in the Saronic Gulf. He rises as if to give a lecture, legs smeared in sand and tunic pressed by sleep. The wagging tails slow to a stop, waiting for their morning speech. Above the sandy bank walks Crates with a jug of water in hand, looking down upon the scene with Diogenes playing teacher to the dogs.

DIOGENES: "Bark, bark!" Diogenes hops up and down. "Bark, bark, bark, ah-hoo!" The dogs all join in.

CRATES: "Playing sophist to the dogs I see," Crates calls out, walking down to offer some water.

DIOGENES: "Well a good cocks crow to you Crates, but dogs need no teaching, only affirmation!"

CRATES: "You really are as mad as everyone says," replies Crates, handing over the jug of water.

DIOGENES: "Only if by mad you mean to judge your own sanity. For I am as mad as this jug of water. And the world is as sane as the sea you see before you. Why don't you go drink both and tell me which tastes more refreshing." Diogenes drinks deeply.

CRATES: "After such witnessing, I must concede I am speechless and shall press no more."

DIOGENES: "Crates, my young pupil, you shall one day see that this world is full of blind men, each willing to persuade you to their sight. Just remember like our friends here, bark at bullshit, snarl at strangers, and howl to Helios every now and again, if nothing else than to say good morning! Now light my lantern. It's time to go to the market to find a good man, shine a light in their eyes, and rouse a little ire."

Midmorning, Diogenes walks along the Cephisus River leading up to the middle wall that connects the harbor of Piraeus to Athens, carrying his lantern and seeding the bank with sand from the folds of his tunic. Crates and the dogs trail close behind. During their walk to the market Diogenes hums a tune normally sung by priests for Apollonesian festivals. Crates posits the connection between Apollo and the light of the lantern.

CRATES: "Teacher, I'm curious about the hymn you now sing and the object of our journey. Is the light of the sun not enough for our eyes to see a good man?

Diogenes stops to consider the question and then proceeds to speak.

DIOGENES: "Look behind you and tell me what you see."

CRATES: "I see the coastal line and the Piraeus peninsula."

DIOGENES: "What do you see below you?"

CRATES: "My feet and sandals, stones and pebbles upon the ground."

DIOGENES: "What do you see in front of you?"

CRATES: "Why you of course."

DIOGENES: "Now take a look at yourself and tell me what you see."

Befuddled, Crates thinks about how he might achieve his teacher's request. He is unable to fulfill the action and supply a response.

DIOGENES: "By the light of Apollo, can't you see yourself? What say you now?

CRATES: "I'm afraid I'm at a loss for words."

DIOGENES: "You asked if day was light enough to see a good man, but maybe you're not a good man. What say you to this?"

CRATES: "I'm sorry but I don't know how to see myself except maybe through still water, Phoenician glass, or polished metal.

DIOGENES: "Dog shit! All you see, if seeing yourself through these, is not a man at all but a sickly image of oneself encased in something one is not. Are you water, glass, or perhaps a metal man? If one were to give one's arm for shake in such a self, would you be able to shake back?"

CRATES: "No, I would not."

DIOGENES: "Then would you agree, if reflections be of this, that one can never truly see oneself?"

CRATES: "It would seem so."

DIOGENES: "But are you able to see me, and I you?"

CRATES: "Yes, of course."

DIOGENES: "Now back to the question at hand. Is there light enough to see a good man? What do you think?"

CRATES: "I would say there is, but why the lantern?"

DIOGENES: "Like your original assumption, Athens has grown full of
    self-reflected swine, consumed, and deluded in reflections of
    golden plates. They paint their face with cosmetics; they dress in
    linen tunics colored in threads for accent; they fall victim to their
    own false reflection. I intend to break their comfortable gaze, stick
    the flame of Apollo in their face, touch everything with my shit-
    wiping left hand, and act as a mirror for true reflection, so that one
    might see themselves for who they truly are! And maybe if we're
    lucky, we'll find one good man. Now come, let us be off."

After 46 stadia of walking, Diogenes and Crates reach the Itonian gate on
the south side of Athens. By the time they reach the market it is close to
noon and Crates is anxious to see what exactly his teacher intends. The
dogs, panting under the sun, begin to sniff their way through the market,
passing Ximenes' leather and sandals, and Archidamus' fine instruments
(lyres of all types and sizes, with discounted five-note flutes of Hermes'
quality). Taking the dogs lead, Diogenes follows the wagging tails.

DIOGENES: "Let's give our friends the first chance to open an
    introduction."

As one might imagine, the dogs manage to find their way to a Phrygian
shopkeeper who specializes in salted and pickled eggs of various broods. A
scribbled sign hangs near the corner of the tent's wooden support, written
in koine Greek, "Best Phrygian Eggs." Diogenes hands his lantern to Crates
and then talks to the dogs. Crates stands off to the side.

DIOGENES: "I know what you mean. It is a good question." The dogs
    begin to bark along with Diogenes. "I don't know. Maybe so, it's
    possible. I can't imagine it so, but I can ask if you'd like?"

At this point, the elderly shopkeeper behind the table is perplexed at
watching this man speaking to dogs and watching the dogs bark back.

SHOPKEEPER: "Phrygian eggs, best Phrygian eggs in Attica. One
      drachma for four.

DIOGENES: "Well that's just it my Phrygian friend, I find . . ."

One of the dogs interrupts loudly with a most aggressive bark.

DIOGENES: "Excuse me. *We* find certain discrepancies surrounding the
      nature of your eggs."

SHOPKEEPER: "What? Best eggs in Attica. No question."

DIOGENES: "Well that's just it. The question stands, as my good friend
      here pointed out, that these eggs could be the best eggs in Attica,
      but close inspection and qualification would be in order for such
      claims of grandeur to be validated. Would you mind allowing me
      the honor of inspecting a few?"

After picking up four of the pickled eggs, Diogenes notices one of his dogs
bent over and proceeding to drop a load of shit in front of the tent. Smiling,
Diogenes continues his inspection, balancing the eggs in both hands,
waiting for his companion to finish his business. After patient timing,
Diogenes turns to his four-legged friend.

DIOGENES: "By the dog! Have you no manners? Look at what you've
      done. This will not do."

SHOPKEEPER: "Damn dog shit near tent, keep customers away!"

Diogenes places the four eggs in his right hand and bends over to pick up
the warm load in his left hand.

SHOPKEEPER: "What you do! What you do! No, give back eggs!"

After throwing the load of shit into the middle of the street, Diogenes continues his inspection, holding all four eggs with both hands and taking in a deep breath, smelling the quality of the eggs.

SHOPKEEPER: "Ahh, disgusting! You gross individual!"

DIOGENES: "I must be honest with you my Phrygian friend. These do not meet the standards of being the best eggs in Attica. They quite smell like shit."

SHOPKEEPER: "You take and go away! Now! Leave! Shew!" Crates is heard laughing in the background.

DIOGENES: "By Zeus! I'd think about changing your sign. The best Phrygian eggs, when not smelling like shit. Good day to you."

Turning away from the shop, Diogenes pops one of the eggs in his mouth and hands one to each of the dogs. Diogenes approaches Crates.

DIOGENES: "Well young Crates, tell me what you saw? Remember first, we can never see ourselves, only others. Thus, we can only learn about ourselves through others. What can we learn of this man, and what insights can we gain for ourselves?"

CRATES: "He did give you the eggs, but he was more concerned about the shit than his eggs. You did disprove the accuracy of his sign, but I'm not sure what more I can learn."

DIOGENES: "Then let me share with you what others might see."

Diogenes bends over to pet one of his fellow companions.

DIOGENES: "Bowel movements should remind all of us of the shit we carry. And whenever you let a person judge you, or in this case, the things you own, as most assuredly will, don't be surprised if they leave shit behind, for even the man who made your tunic wiped his ass on more than one occasion."

About to continue his response, Diogenes briefly pauses, distracted by three young Dionysian priestesses appearing to be on errands for the temple, each one walking his way.

DIOGENES: "And finally, Crates, if a woman should look upon you as a proper lover, the shit we face in life only becomes compounded!"

Not aware of his teacher's distraction, Crates follows up with additional questions.

CRATES: "Is there a remedy to this? How are we to avoid such conditions?"

Grabbing Crates shoulders as a father might embrace his son before a hug, Diogenes looks into Crates' eyes.

DIOGENES: "A good man embraces the shit of others, if only just to return the favor."

Once removing his hands, Crates is left with the salty smell of vinegar on his right shoulder, with a brown handprint on his left. Diogenes approaches the young priestesses as someone might with a secret beckoning to be shared and looking to give confession.

DIOGENES: "By the vine!"

Diogenes points to the decorated jugs in two of the girls' hands, each clay molding smoothed over in a white coat and adorned with vine-like details. No doubt a temple-issued artisan crafted each jug, for hidden symbols of the religious occult are inscribed within each vine, making even the best educated Athenian turn a browed-eye to recall Homer or Hesiod for reference.

DIOGENES: "Young ladies of Bacchus, I do believe, with holy wine for trade for those who might pay tribute for the Theban man made divine by the princess Semele and our beloved Zeus!"

The eldest priestess, who appears to be leading their market errand, steps forward to address Diogenes, slightly cautious of strangers but secure with stature to speak as a temple priestess.

ELDER: "We are as you say, Bacchus' brides, and must warn, Maenad-minded should words intend. But I see you speak with holy truth, for it is true Semele and Zeus being the origin of our love, and sweet wine the lips we kiss. What, might I ask, may we do for you should tributes portend?"

Each of the three priestesses proceed to bow, customary of devote servitude.

DIOGENES: "Well, seeing such priestesses as the three of you, I felt compelled to share a tale I heard and find your thoughts on the matter."

ELDER: "Proceed and we shall share our opinion."

DIOGENES: "I once knew a tavern owner in my travels through Ionia. One night, this owner shared a most remarkable tale with me—by Zeus—he swore it to be true. The tavern had been in his family for many generations. Four to be exact. The tale begins there, before the current owner was born. It was the end of spring, and soon to rise Adonis' red anemone. In walked a man like never he saw. He sat down at the end of the bar, near the empty jars the owner had just recently set upon to clean before refilling. When the man went to reach for one of the jars, the owner politely shared their hollowness, but the man picked up the jar and poured anyways. The owner walked down to inspect. To his surprise, all of the empty jars were now full and smelled of the sweetest wine he had ever smelled."

All three of the dogs sit patiently by their master's side, but one decides to chime in at this moment of the story, barking for attention.

DIOGENES: "Please excuse my impatient friend," Diogenes spoke to the priestesses before turning to his companion, "I'm getting to the point my good friend."

To the elder's left, one of the priestess giggles in watching Diogenes speak to the dog.

DIOGENES: "As one might suppose, this tavern owner's great, great grandfather made praise for this Dionysian miracle! The stranger raised his glass with a smile and spoke with words that apparently bless all who might discern and live by its truth. Have you happened to have heard this tale?"

All three of the priestesses are thoroughly captivated, for none had heard this tale before.

ELDER: "We most certainly have not, but quite believe the authenticity, for the God of Wine works in all corners of Hellena and beyond. Many stories, unless shared, go un- recounted."

DIOGENES: "For a glass of holy wine, I shall finish the tale that my tavern friend shared with me."

Diogenes pulls a wooden cup from under his tunic, strapped by a cross thread of cloth. The elder signals to one of the priestess to pour a glass for Diogenes, and signals the other to sing the traditional hymn.

PRIESTESSES: "O Bacchanals, come,

Oh, come.
Sing Dionysus,
Sing to the timbrel,
The deep-voiced timbrel. Joyfully praise him,
Him who brings joy.
Holy, all holy
Music is calling.
To the hills, to the hills, Fly,
O Bacchanal
Swift of foot.
On, O joyful, be fleet.[1]"

The priestess finishes the blessing with imparting a kiss to Diogenes. Stepping back away from him, the priestess' nose twitches with the subtle hint of shit and vinegar.

ELDER: "Come now, please continue your tale for we have shared our wine and given holy blessings unto you."

Diogenes is smiling from ear to ear. The dogs notice their master's happy state and wag their tails with frenzy.

DIOGENES: "Tis true, a holy blessing you've given, for I feel its affects already and drink in gulps for hopes of more."

Diogenes winks to the priestess in the back.

DIOGENES: "Well, as I was saying, this stranger gave a most beautiful blessing. I remember the words well, for the great, great grandfather later inscribed the blessing at the back of the bar as a sort of sanctification and blessing for all travelers who drink at his tables. The stranger spoke these words.

STRANGER: 'Nature's fruit grows all around but starts of soil upon the ground. Take heed to bless with hands of earth and honor the cup for times of mirth.'

DIOGENES: "This, I confess, the owner shared with me, and now I share with you, for blessings should be shared, and I thank you for sharing yours."

Diogenes returns a salutary bow to the priestesses. Seeing this the dogs begin to bark with fury, thinking this gesture a game signaled by their teacher.

ELDER: "We thank you for the blessing, knowing the fruits of the vine work in mysterious ways, and surely these words will cross-pollinate Hellena and beyond. Before we part and bid goodbye, I must say, you really should tie up your dogs before they bite someone!"

DIOGENES: "Don't worry me lady, my dog is securely tied down and only bites when beckoned too!"

Diogenes unties his tunic to flash the young ladies with his dog knot. He gives a jingle with a thrust of the hips. The younger priestesses' blush red from the provocative display. The elder pushes past Diogenes and continues down the market, regretting her final words.

DIOGENES: "By the dog! I believe you're right me lady. The vine really works in mysterious ways. I feel it now! Bark! Bark! Aw-hoo!"

All the dogs join in, howling and barking, as Diogenes unties his dog knot and beats away at his own third leg. One of the priestess, who earlier giggled at his ability to talk with the dogs, now looks back and sends a smile his way. Diogenes calls out to her with only one hand free.

DIOGENES: "I shall send additional blessings your way later tonight, behind the Stoa in the Agora should you like to reciprocate!"

Once again, Crates is heard laughing in the background. Before Crates could approach his teacher, a wealthy Athenian walks by leering at Diogenes' indecency. Diogenes gives a response to his viewing:

DIOGENES: "Good sir, I only wish I could satisfy my hunger in similar manner, rubbing my stomach with equal enthusiasm!"

The wealthy Athenian walks away without saying a word. Crates approaches his teacher, still holding the lantern.

CRATES: "Tis truly a marvelous sight to see your teaching."

DIOGENES: "Let me be the judge."

Diogenes proceeds to refit his tunic. The dogs circle around.

DIOGENES: "What have you learned?"

CRATES: "I watched you infuriate a merchant with hands of shit, discredit the truth of his claim and obtain a free lunch. I watched you charm three priestesses with words, being blessed and blessing in return, achieving holy wine. And finally, making full display of the masturbation within the market, helping others to see the source of their own vanities."

Diogenes listens to his young companion's recapitulation, almost half-heartedly, wishing his pupil could see more than what he has shared.

DIOGENES: "I worry you do not follow my leading as carefully as I would like. Let us continue walking."

Both Crates and Diogenes walk at a slow pace as they proceed through the market.

DIOGENES: "Look around yourself. Do you see how people stare at you, holding a lit lantern in broad daylight?"

CRATES: "I do, for many have been staring for quite some time."

DIOGENES: "Carrying a lantern is no extraordinary thing, would you agree?"

CRATES: "I would."

DIOGENES: "But why do you suspect they stare?"

CRATES: "I do not know."

DIOGENES: "They stare for what you represent. Uncertainty. What man carries a lit lantern in broad daylight? No one does, and so you represent uncertainty. They cannot conceive of the why, and for what reason you carry this fire. They stare and contemplate, achieving inward reflection through another man's action—*your actions*."

Diogenes pauses to let this last line sink in.

DIOGENES: "Let me ask you this, what was the original purpose of our trip?"

CRATES: "To find a good man."

DIOGENES: "Yes, good. Now what I have not told you is why we are searching for a good man, but we will get to that soon enough. Early, you witnessed the disgust of one man's encounter with another man's shit. He withdrew in horror, sacrificing his own property to avoid the touch."

DIOGENES: "A good man embraces the shit of others, always mindful of the load he carries himself."

CRATES: "This is true."

DIOGENES: "Secondly, you observed me bearing witness to three priestesses' self-reflection, for the truth I shared was no more than giving back to the truth they already hold. The golden sophist from Leontini, as I'm sure you know, might call my actions apate or possibly a good verbal example of doxa entwined in holy logos of the god Dionysus."

CRATES: "I know of Gorgias and see the connection of what you say."

DIOGENES: "Good. Now, as we earlier discussed, Athens is plagued by false reflections. Once aware, the art of persuasion, one might say, is the simple conjuring of identification." One of the dogs nuzzles up next to Diogenes' leg. "Yes, I know, I am almost finished."

CRATES: "But teacher, if what you say is true, why did you reinforce the priestesses' self-reflection?"

DIOGENES: "Why Crates, some reflections are truly beautiful, especially when they give sweet wine and kisses. The gods have truly blessed us."

Diogenes winks at Crates.

DIOGENES: "But your question is well grounded and needs further explanation. Like the man who gave witness to my bareness, we saw the uncertainty in his eyes turned into a wicked leer of ill will."

CRATES: "Very true, I almost thought he was going to engage you in physical dispute."

DIOGENES: "And did you notice the eyes of his judgment? The man truly abhorred the self-reflection of what he believed one could only do in private."

CRATES: "What you say is quite true."

DIOGENES: "And in this way Crates, we are our brother's keeper. In this time of great delusions, one must help remind humanity of our common nature, base as it might be—'tis still better than chains of lies. And for this reason they call me a cynic, student of Antisthenes from the school of Cynosarges. Let them call me, 'Socrates gone mad.' I know we are no better than dogs—and I intend to keep the truth in full view."

CRATES: "If the goal is to be this vehicle of awakening, I'm curious about why we are in 'search for a good man' if knowing the current state we live in? Shouldn't our goal be to break as many people from the bonds of their own self-delusion?"

DIOGENES: "Good. Crates, are you familiar with the Oracle of Delphi's inscription to 'Know Thyself'?"

CRATES: "Why certainly, it is a story shared to most children."

DIOGENES: "Good. Now let me ask, what makes a good ship builder?"

CRATES: "Someone who makes good ships?"

DIOGENES: "Yes. Now, what makes a good politician?"

CRATES: "Someone who makes good decisions for the city?"

DIOGENES: "Yes. Now, what makes a good architect?"

CRATES: "Someone who makes good, strong structures."

DIOGENES: "Now, what do each share in common?"

CRATES: "They each strive after the good?"

DIOGENES: "Yes. Quite right. Now do you agree with the Oracle that one ought to know thyself?"

CRATES: "Most certainly."

DIOGENES: "Do you agree that one's reflection is distorted by mirrors, metal, gold, cosmetics, and other fineries that mask a person, so that true reflection may only stem from another?"

CRATES: "I most certainly agree."

DIOGENES: "Why then, the search for a good man should be clear. Each searches after the good in their profession. If we are to be our brother's keeper, our goal should always be in search of a good man. In this pursuit, with Apollo's light, we might know ourselves and help others reflect inward. In this way we may all apprehend true self-reflection!"

After speaking these words, Diogenes stops in the middle of the market with a smile on his face. To his right, a small child is seen drinking water with cupped hands from the public fountain. Diogenes reaches for his cup beneath his tunic. To Crates surprise, Diogenes drops the cup upon the ground and proceeds to join the young boy for a drink of water.

NOTES
1. The Bacchanal hymn comes from Edith Hamilton's *Mythology*.

About the Author

Steven M. Pedersen is a collector of false starts, failed paths, and fool's errands. His career began at Jack-in-the-Box in high school, working the drive-thru lane and handing out extra ranch sauce to his favorite customers. He later made a splash at SeaWorld in the entertainment department, overseeing shows and flirting with animal trainers and costume characters. His father would call him "Stevo, the Shamu man," before later calling him "Stevo, the Beer man," after he got a job with Coors selling beer in Los Angeles and expensing bar rounds on the company's dime. Between then and now, he's been a door-to-door solar salesman in Denver and a broker for a third-party logistics company managing freight across the US. He has never been married, but he has been divorced.

Despite these meanderings, he has managed to finish an MA in English and a PhD in Composition, Rhetoric, and Technical Writing. His work can be found in Rhetoric Review, The Kenneth Burke Journal, the Journal of the American Studies Association of Texas, and The Oklahoman. He currently lives in Ada, Oklahoma, where he teaches writing and "what not to do" in the classrooms at East Central University.

His pursuit in poetry is motivated by hopes of absolution.